MY LAST NAME IS
GRANDMA

ELLA ELLIOTT COLVIN

Copyright © 2022 Ella Elliott Colvin.

All rights reserved. No part of this book may be reproduced, stored, or transmitted by any means—whether auditory, graphic, mechanical, or electronic—without written permission of both publisher and author, except in the case of brief excerpts used in critical articles and reviews. Unauthorized reproduction of any part of this work is illegal and is punishable by law.

ISBN: 979-8-88640-577-4 (sc)
ISBN: 979-8-88640-578-1 (hc)
ISBN: 979-8-88640-579-8 (e)

Because of the dynamic nature of the Internet, any web addresses or links contained in this book may have changed since publication and may no longer be valid. The views expressed in this work are solely those of the author and do not necessarily reflect the views of the publisher, and the publisher hereby disclaims any responsibility for them.

One Galleria Blvd., Suite 1900, Metairie, LA 70001
1-888-421-2397

This book is dedicated to all Grandparents,
but especially to our Grandkid's other Grandparents,
who like us, have created an unbreakable bond with them.

CONTENTS

Prologue vii
These Two 1
Sisters Laughing 3
Who Does What and When? 5
It's My Turn 7
Red Light Green Light 9
Less is Good 11
Popsicles 13
What I Learned at Pre-School 15
Let Me Tell You About Her 17
Overnight Stays 19
Don't Deny Papa His Joy 22
Oops! Excuse Me, I burped 24
I Don't Like Chili's 27
Going To Church 29
Grandma He's Speeding Again 32
At Granny's House 34
What Does That Mean? 37
Epilogue 41
About the Author 41

PROLOGUE

When my Husband and I became Grandparents, we were surprised at the uncontrollable and endless flow of love and affection we felt for our Grandkids. It was a feeling that seem to equal or surpass the feelings we had for our children when they were growing up (sorry kids). But we soon found that while the love seemed to be as equal, it wasn't. We were much more expressive. Before we became grandparents, we often saw other grandparents with their grandkids, and wondered what all the fuss was about. Well, we have six, and now understand that once grandkids arrive there is this overpowering invisible connection that develops. It was a connection that my Maternal Grandmother had (I never knew my Paternal Grandmother). I believe that my Maternal Grandmother (Granny as she was called) was the litmus test, the gold standard for all Grandmothers. She showered all of her grandkids with unconditional love and made each of us feel as if we were the most important person in the world. When my family visited our Maternal Grandparents, and my Grandpa's house, it was the highlight of our young lives. I knew Granny as Granny, and I am sure that I didn't learn her last name until I was much older. To me her name could have been Granny, No Middle Initial, Granny, because to us it was about the way she made us feel, and how we felt about her, and the name Granny was all we needed to know. My grandkids call me Grandma, and for the longest time that was all they knew, and I didn't mind at all.

My Husband and I feel blessed that we are able to witness the making of this generation. I consider it a privilege to share just a small portion of what they have to offer. My hope is that their other Grandparents will get a glimpse of what we have been afforded, and on these pages experience the laughter, love and joy of "Our Grandkids".

THESE TWO

Our grandkids are a part of the Z, or silent, or internet generation and it is an awesome feeling to be a part of that legacy. While raising our kids, they were not always receptive to all the traditions that we tried to pass down from our parents. I now take joy in passing them to our grandkids. My husband and I have four that live within 3 miles of us. The older two of the four have provided me with numerous opportunities to share and contribute to the outcome of their upbringing. It has been enlightening to watch each child teach the next child what they have learned from their parents, grandparents, each other and others. These Two together were a book waiting to be written, and I am just touching the surface of their lives.

The older of the two, KeeKee, was the first grandchild I saw being born. Being a nurse, I had seen and helped with many births, but watching your own grandchild come into the world is totally different. That birth got me hooked on grandkids! As with most "first born" everyone showered her with love, affection and the gift of knowledge. She was introduced to music, reading, math, French and computers early, and as a result she has great reasoning and memory skills. KeeKee has shown us that the attention she was given early in life has produced a very smart and talented girl. She tells us that she is shy, but she is openly affectionate, very strong willed, and she is an advocate of "boy power."

The younger of the two TraTra, was very sickly as a baby. I remember that she cried a lot as a baby and a toddler. Just as she was very loud with her crying, she is still using her voice, but in an imaginative way. TraTra is very outgoing and creative, and can make up a song, or a poem about anything: literally anything. Tiny framed with the energy of a hurricane; she is an advocate of "girl power." She constantly asked: why is Grandma doing all the work? I like this girl power!

The two of them spend a lot of time together, and as they grew, we could see their distinctive personalities. Their sisterly bond was, and is strong, and it showed when they were in trouble as they looked out for each during those times. Like my sisters and I, they have created a bond that will carry them through their child and adulthood.

SISTERS LAUGHING

Growing up with my Sisters produced a bond that carried "US" through our childhood, and made us even closer in our adulthood. Raised poor, we discovered that we could create fun by using simple things like strings to make pretend houses, and dirt to make food. Our times together made memories that we still laugh about today.

Each of us had different personalities, different ways of doing things, and we had different dreams for our future. While we all took varied roads, one common bond was the fun we shared. When we get together, one thing that we always share is Sisters Laughing.

When I was a kid growing up, my vision for the future included having a husband, ten kids, and a two-story house with a picket fence (what kind of books was I reading). I craved that kind of life, because of all the fun I had growing up. Even though our family lived on a farm, and we were poor, we had things that money could not buy, home grown food, fun, and family. Our parents raised us based on how they were raised, and it was driven by Biblical principles.

I grew up with three sisters (I have four), one brother, and we claim a cousin as our brother too. My Father was the playful one, and my Mother was more of the disciplinarian. We were all close growing up, and now as adults share in the joy, and sorrows of our kids and grandkids.

I do not remember grandkids being part of my daydreaming when I was 16, but since my sisters, and I have become Grandparents, we have lots of stories to share. The stories we impart to each other really validates that our children are normal, and that our children, and grandchildren are great discussion tools. My sisters and I have spent many times on the phone discussing and laughing about our situations. That fun and joy we shared as kids continues through our kids and grandchildren. We have discovered that while life has many turns and twist, joys and sorrows, the situations usually are the same with different names or families. Often times I would call one of my sisters wanting to vent about something that was going on with the kids, or grandkids, and we would end up discussing the day's happenings. In the mist of our frustration and sharing, we found that by the end of the conversation our laughter had overtaken the situation that prompted the call: that same laughter that reminded us of our childhood. Most of the laughter was usually about ……… We'll never tell. Let the laughter between Sisters continue.

WHO DOES WHAT AND WHEN?

Where did parents get their guidelines that indicated when someone was old enough to do certain things? When did maturity outweigh age? Well, it didn't happen during my Baby Boomer generation, which included people born between 1947 and 1967. My parents literally stuck to their beliefs about their kids having to be a certain age to do things throughout our childhood.

When my husband and I raised our kids, we used some of the age gages we grew up with, but we also busted the mold on some of those traditions. While helping to raise our grandkids, we found that they were much smarter, and some of those gages didn't work. We decided to use age and maturity as our gage to determine, Who Does What and When.

Some adults continue to use age as their gage to indicate when people should be allowed to do certain things. For example, when I was growing up, I could not date until I was 16. I could cut my hair one time, but I had to be 16 to do that too.

We told our Grandkids that because we were older, that only Grandmothers, Grandpas, Moms, Dads, Aunts and Uncles could use a knife, turn the stove on, pick them up from school, etc., etc. We also told them that only Grandmothers, Moms, or Aunts could wash their private parts. As they were processing the information, one of the girls asked, what about Granny (my Mom). Can she wash us too? I quickly added her to the wash list.

Kids are taught their age early in life and can repeat it when asked. I didn't believe that they had any real concept of age-related gages, until the older of the two, KeeKee, proclaimed one day; Grandma is older than Papa, but Papa is taller. These comments from her showed me that she did understand the concept of age, and she used it in such a way that indicated that both her grandparents had good qualities. I believe she was indicating that Grandma was older, and she could do certain things, but Papa was taller, and he could do certain things. It was little nuggets of information like this from KeeKee that highlighted her thinking, and reasoning at an early age. She was perhaps suggesting that it was not always about how old you are, but about the qualities that the person has that enables them to do certain things. So as we decide who should do what, and when at what age, we should look at the capabilities of the person. This will be very beneficial as their generation enters the work force. They will be younger, and I believe much smarter in certain areas than the Baby Boomers, Generation X, (the generation after the baby boomers), and Generation Y, (the ones after the Xers). So many of us may have to change our thinking about age related capabilities being the driving force behind who does what and when. The ability of KeeKee to see each grandparent's quality reminds me of someone who speaks politically correct. If politics is in her future, she is starting early!

IT'S MY TURN

I wanted to believe that growing up my brothers, and sisters did not always use schemes to promote something for themselves. I wanted to believe that what they did was for the good of all of us. I also wanted to believe that when everyone encouraged me to take their turn to ride a chainless bike with my eyes closed while they pushed me, that they were being nice, and had no ulterior motive (that was not the case!). Just as me and my siblings maneuvered situations to get ahead, or have fun at the expense of each other, we are finding that our grandkids are using tactics to help themselves get ahead as well. They learned that going first had its advantages, so will try anything to be able to say, It's My Turn.

Listening to our grandkids talk to each other, I realized that they, like my siblings, were always scheming or competing with one another to determine who's better, who goes first, or gets the fullest cup? KeeKee occasionally reminded TraTra that she went first last week, and it is her turn now. However, she learned early that she could get "cookie points" if she let TraTra go first. "Grandma, I am letting her go before me because she is the youngest." This made her look good and may have gotten her extra goodies. But most of the time, she will ask TraTra, do you want to go first or last? If you go first, then I will be last. If you go last then, I will be first. The youngest usually chooses to go first, and the oldest shouts, "I always have to go last"! TraTra yells, "Grandma, she won't let me go first."

Enter the wisdom of grand parenting. "Everyone has to share going first. If one goes first this time, the other one goes first next time." This seemed to be a simple solution. The only problem is that you, the grandparent had to develop a system that helped you remember who went first last time. You had to remember who you gave food to first, who got in or out of the car first, or who you said good night to first. Believe me, they remember! I believe this is a good place to interject the "notion" that one should give the older grandchild more berries than the younger one without the younger finding out and feeling bad. I believe this can be accomplished up until the younger one can count. After that, I suggest giving everyone equal amounts, or maybe use a non-see through bowl for the oldest. Of course, KeeKee will sometime shout out, I got the most, and grandma served me first. This should put an end to the idea that the oldest gets more or goes first because they are the oldest.

Watching the two of them battle over who goes first, or decide whose turn it is, I let them solve their own conflict sometimes as it develops their negotiating skills. A good indicator that I needed to get involved was the familiar cry from one of them, "Grandma it's my turn and she won't let me go first".

RED LIGHT GREEN LIGHT

When I am driving, and come upon a traffic light, I have decided that I would rather come upon a red light rather than a green one. Red because I know I have to stop. A green light indicates that I may have to get ready to stop, or I might not make it through the intersection. A red light gives my brain a rest from having to make a decision about traffic lights. Our Grandkids took a totally different approach to the traffic lights. The more lights that change colors the better they liked it, because for them, it was game of colors: Red Light Green Light.

Traffic signal lights are a great way to teach grandkids colors, and it keeps them busy when traveling. As we travel down the road, they play a game that allows one child to say one of the colors on the traffic signal. They eventually developed their own way of determining who would say what color when we approached the light. KeeKee indicated to TraTra, yesterday, you said red light, so I say red light today, green light tomorrow, and yellow light on Wednesday. Today you say yellow light, red light tomorrow, and then green light. Grandma, do you want to say red light, green light? The answer should always be NO!

As grandparents, you do not want your memory tested, especially when you drive through hundreds of traffic lights when traveling. I am still trying to remember who I gave orange juice to first this morning. I am not going to add another memory exercise to my brain. It really is good to have young minds with great memory skills. We have used those memory skills to locate remotes, keys, books, etc. They remember everything. My husband put a number lock on our front door. It really is a nice keyless addition to the house. Of course, KeeKee, the older grandchild has memorized the combination, and has mentioned it out loud on occasion. After a brief discussion of the consequences of unwanted intruders, she finally understood that a show of her memory skills is not always appropriate when people are around. She learned that her memory skill should not be displayed at certain times. Good memory has pros and cons, and as my husband, and I mature in age, I am beginning to believe that the pros outnumber the cons. We can always change our keyless number combination. The memory building skills they are obtaining and using (even red light green light) will help them with the memory challenges (such as spelling test), that they will face in their life.

LESS IS GOOD

I do not know of many instances where less could be considered good. I believe that we walk in the Spirit humbly with our God, and that the meek shall inherit the earth. Isaiah 60:22 states that a little one shall become a thousand, and a small one a strong one: I the Lord will hasten it in his time. In that sense less is good. In the earthly realm, it would take some creativity for someone to convince me that Less Is Good.

I believe that every grandparent has a "great story" to tell about their grandkids. I also believe that every grandparent believes that their grandkids are the smartest, and the prettiest. Well, we are no different. I was amazed at the wisdom grandkids displayed early in their lives. Their thought process is very young, and you have to wonder how they are able to figure things out at such an early age. KeeKee and TraTra were five and three years old, and were eating dinner at our house one night, when KeeKee, the oldest began a conversation with TraTra, that really showed their early development. She stated, "I have some good news, and I have some bad news for you. The good news is that you are beating me eating. The bad news is that you have less food. Because you have less food you are beating me, which means I have more than you."

TraTra happily proclaimed with a smile, "Grandma, Grandma, I've got less!" Indicating she had the winning hand. "Grandparents, wasn't she too young to be thinking like that?" I am still wondering how she was able to put those concepts together, and then put them into a scenario that made the younger one feel good. KeeKee showed great reasoning skills early, but I was always amazed every time I saw her using that skill. I am sure that she uses it when she wants to get ahead. But it appears she had a way of not making the other person feel bad about it.

Our daughter mentioned just recently that when she talks to KeeKee or ask her a question she stares at her for a few minutes without answering her. My daughter indicated that her teacher had noticed that she also does that at school. I believe I understand why she pauses, or stares before she answers. She is thinking of all the ways she can answer the question, and make it a win-win for all. We have asked her not to stare at the person when she is asked a question. We have asked her to say "I'm thinking" so that the person would not think she is being rude, by not answering right away. I hope we are not interrupting her thinking process. Anyone who can make someone feel good about having less must be allowed to utilize their reasoning ability to the fullest.

POPSICLES

"Mommy, where do babies come from?" I believe that was the most intriguing question that we asked when I was growing up. Answers to questions like these were vague or ambiguous at the most. It seems that this generation of grandkids is looking at simple things to build their knowledge base. I have eaten many Popsicles, and I don't think I ever wondered where they came from. Answering questions from KeeKee and TraTra gave my husband and I a sense of pride that one's wisdom is being passed from person to person, even if it is about a simple thing like Popsicles.

"Grandma, why do they call Popsicles, Popsicles?" What Grandparent knows the answer to this question! I promised to look it up, and let the grandkids know. It had been about a month, when I was asked "Grandma did you find out why Popsicles are called Popsicles?" I had not so I went online and discovered how Popsicles got their name. Grandparents please remember this, as you may be asked.

Once upon a time, a little boy was drinking a pop. I explained to the girls that we called, a soda, a pop. A pop is a sugary flavored drink that comes in a bottle, and it could be an Orange, Grape, or another favorite drink. The little boy put a stick in his pop and left it outside.

The pop froze with the stick inside, and when he pulled the stick out, the pop was frozen on the stick. This pop on a stick was first called the "Epicicle", after the family name, but later the name was changed to "Popsicle".

Questions like this began early, and it is so important that parents and grandparents get it right. These little tidbits are repeated and passed down to the younger grandkids in the backseat as you travel to school or while traveling on vacation. Hearing your wisdom or knowledge being passed down gives you a warm feeling that generational learning goes on. I don't remember if we got the kind of questions from our kids that our grandkids ask. As parents we were always rushing to get somewhere and may have missed a lot of those back seat questions, hence missing more opportunities to teach or to learn from our kids.

I really cherish all the times I have had the opportunity to be a driver or a passenger with the grandkids riding in the back. Not only are they exploring the passing world, but they have a way of bringing excitement to a road that I have seen a million times. The beauty of fresh eyes remind us of how innocent their world begins. It is sad that we can't "can" that innocence, and when we feel they need it, just pop it open and start over.

WHAT I LEARNED AT PRE-SCHOOL

I never attended a daycare, or a preschool as a child. My first entrance into a school system was first grade. I enjoyed going to school, as it was a way of escaping from the farm work at home. I remember reading books as a way to fill the void of boredom, and as a way to discover answers to the questions that weren't answered at school or home. Kids today are entering learning settings earlier and absorbing information much faster. Our job is to be open to opportunities to add to that knowledge. My belief is that learning never ceases, and we can all learn any time and any place, even at Pre-School.

My husband and I spent about three months doing the "school run" for my daughter. She was pregnant with her third child and spent the majority of her time on bed rest. I picked up the two grandkids from their home and took them to pre-school. She later moved in with us when her pregnancy became more difficult. What an opportunity to bond, answer questions, learn, teach, and say I don't know, but Grandma will find out. What an opportunity to use smoothies, pop tarts, pancakes, and gum bribes (don't tell their Mom) to get things done.

At pre-school one day, one of the girl's classmates asked me my name. I told her my name, and a couple of days later the classmate stated, that she had forgotten my name, and ask if I could tell her again. I told her my first name with a Mrs. tag. Another classmate asked for my last name. Before I could tell her my last name, TraTra said "her last name is Grandma." KeeKee immediately spoke up and told the classmates my last name. I heard TraTra recite my last name with the other students in unison as if it was the first time, she had ever heard it. As they were speaking, I realized that I was the one in the learning mode at school that day. Just when you thought you had discussed all the simple and basic things with them, we had overlooked one thing: last names. Are first and last names really important to grandkids when they are young? The terms grandma and grandpa or whatever terms are used, create a feeling within the grandparents that is blissful when they hear it. When someone ask us to explain that feeling, most of us are at a loss for words. When TraTra stated that my last name was Grandma, I didn't mind at all. She was validating that unexplainable feeling that we have as grandparents. To her my first name was Grandma, and my last name was Grandma.

Regardless, part of my role is teaching, so on the ride home that day; we began the discussion of last names.

LET ME TELL YOU ABOUT HER

    I have tried to live by the saying, "don't judge a book by its cover", and have tried to give people the benefit of the doubt when I first meet them. While first impressions are sometimes a good indicator of that person, I realize that this is not always the case. Kids tend to listen and watch how adults treat and talk to people. Some of them base their perception of that person on what they have seen and heard. Having kids see the world through adult eyes is an awesome responsibility. We try to project a positive learning experience while trying to hide our biases about certain situations. Telling somebody about somebody can easily color their opinion, because it is based on yours and not their perception. I learned that kids gather information and store it for later use, and when they need it, pull it out of somewhere to share what they know. Let Me Tell You About Her was one example of this stored information.

    I believe that at an early age children develop their opinion about someone based on how that person treats them. I also believe that most kids will forget hurt feelings, give people the benefit of the doubt, and not hold grudges. When playing, they appear to have anger or frustration for a little while, and then pick up where they left off. At least that is what I thought. I picked up the grandkids from Summer School, and they were telling me about their day. TraTra reported that Meale had pushed her, and made her hurt her leg. In an effort to determine who had hurt her little sister, KeeKee, asked, "which Meale was it? Was it Meale Jones or Meale Johns? What does she look like? Meale Jones' hair sticks out like this (using her hand to demonstrate)." "It was Meale Jones", states TraTra. KeeKee began to further proclaim, "well she is not a nice person." Meale Johns is nice, and she would not do that. Thus began the stage of older sister protecting the little sister and passing down impressions she developed about someone. Using that information, she had stored for later use, and that her little sister will use to judge Meale Jones. We have watched the older grandchild share with her little sisters what she has learned from everyone as she was growing up. We have to wonder if she has heard or seen us make a judgment about someone, without also letting her see the forgiveness part. As we watch the older child display such pride in teaching the younger ones, she easily gets offended when they do not listen to her wisdom. Wisdom and advice at five years old that she believes is "tried and true" and should be listened to.

OVERNIGHT STAYS

Visits to any grandparent's house are usually an experience that most kids cherish. When I visited my Granny's house, our fun and memories were made during the day, as we did not get to stay overnight very often. My Father believed that we would have been an imposition to our Granny, and he did not want her to over work herself looking after grandkids. So when it was time to go home, our goodbyes were full of tears. We took the fun we had and put it into our memory bank for warm fuzzes when we needed a boost. A visit to our Granny's house gave it to us every time.

Most grandkids love staying at Grandma and Grandpa's house, and the same is true about most grandparents: they loved having the grandkids stay at their house. Our grandkids are no exception as they asked to stay almost every day. When they visited or stayed it gave us an opportunity to do those things that we didn't do, or did not have the opportunity to do with our own kids. We got to do those things that were forbidden with our own kids. I believe that being a grandparent gives you a free pass to do the things with your grandkids that you learned while rearing your own children, and now know that it didn't kill them. Grandparents have learned how to have fun without the boundaries of shouldn't and cants. I have heard my own daughter say, "We couldn't do that when we were kids." She is absolutely right.

I believe, I finally know why we-grandparents-do, and act the way we do in regard to our grandkids. As parents we were entering into unknown territories. We were raising kids based on how we were raised. We had to learn that kids can go outside and run safely without falling down and breaking a leg. We had to learn that kids can fall down the stairs and survive. We had to learn that it is OK to go to sleep at night while they are sleeping. We learned these things raising our own kids. Our grandkids are the playing field for this knowledge. We are able to relax and enjoy helping our daughter with her kids without all the fear we had with our own. Some new parents have not arrived at this stage, so find themselves going through parenthood like everyone else: limited in the enjoyment of parenthood.

As Baby Boomers raising Generation X kids, we did spoil our kids. We raised them in the era where our lifestyle was a little better than our parents. Most of our parents could only provide us with things we needed. We made sure that our kids had all the things that we did not have when we were kids. Most Baby Boomers were labeled as spoilers of their kids, but spoiling Grandkids is a whole different ball game.

The grandkids learned early that good things happen at their Grandparents' house, or when their other Grandparents come to visit. Grandkids get: read to (a lot), ice cream in their Oatmeal instead of milk, later bed times, bed snacks of hot tea in tiny cups, taken to the fair, get to visit fancy hotels with special events (duck walk), and adult playmates that actually play with them on the floor. TraTra appreciated all those niceties early in the evening, but at bedtime she wanted to go home to her Mommy. After the phone call to Mommy, the crying, the holding, she finally resigned herself to staying the entire night. Grandma assured her that she would take her home in the morning.

The next morning after they were dressed, and ready to go home, she gives Grandma a big leg hug and states "Thank you Grandma for letting us go home". Years later, when the girls stayed at Grandma and Papa's house, there is no mention of going home in the middle of the night. Now we use "we are going to take you home" as a deterrent to bad behavior.

DON'T DENY PAPA HIS JOY

 Some of the greatest joy in the world comes from the birth of a child, and the birth of a grandchild. Fathers and Grandfathers who experience this joy began to develop their own way of expressing their happiness. While Mothers are known for their outward show of affection and love, it caught me off guard when the grandfather in my husband matched the grandmother in me. It took me a while to step aside and let him enjoy being a grandfather in his own way as I was a grandmother in my own way. I learned that to Deny Papa his Joy resulted in frustration for him, and less joy for our grandkids.

 When I was growing up, my Daddy was the parent who provided us with the most fun in our household. He was the playful one: the one who would get down on the floor and play with us. My Mom was more of the disciplinarian, who spent most of her time trying to get us to do the right thing, which was a full-time job! Our grandkids that live the closest call their Grandfather, Papa, and he is a very hands-on grandparent. They have benefited from his involvement with them, and as I watched Him with them, I could see the pride, and love he had for them. I could see the joy he felt as he interacted with them, whether playing games, fixing a meal, helping them with homework or a project. He often commented that he wishes our grandchildren who do not live as close were closer, so we could spend more time with them. As I watched him with the grandkids, I found myself saying to him, "they don't need that, or that's too much, or you shouldn't do that. One day I came downstairs, and the grandkids were eating freshly popped popcorn from his new movie style popcorn popper, applesauce, and they had a juice box. I asked them where they had gotten the food. They responded proudly in unison, "Papa". I asked Papa, why he had given them popcorn, applesauce and a juice box (I am thinking to myself, what a combination). He replied, "They wanted it".

As I think back to our own children's childhood, I thought of their grandparents, aunts, and uncles. In their early years, they spent most of their time near their paternal grandmother. They got to know their maternal grandparents on visits to their farm during our vacation time. My daughter would tell us stories of things their paternal grandmother, great aunts, aunt and uncle did that they knew we would never have done. Hence the cycle continues. We now have the opportunity to continue that cycle of forbidden "spoiling". When we were raising our own kids, we were so busy providing our kids mostly with things we thought they should have, because we did not have them, that we did not always give them the fun things that Grandparents gave them. As Grandparents, we have reversed our actions: kids get mainly what they need, and grandkids get what they want. Standing in the way of Papa's joy is Grandma. Who am I to deprive Papa of the same joy Grandma gets fulfilling wants instead of needs? I have come to understand that there are very little differences in the degree of pride, joy and affection between grandparent genders. So, Grandmas should keep as quiet as possible when Grandpas are exercising their rights as a Grandparent, even if it is a meal of popcorn, applesauce, and a juice box.

OOPS! EXCUSE ME, I BURPED

I was taught to say yes and no ma'am, yes and no sir, excuse me or oops I'm sorry. Using these words often indicated that you had good manners. My husband and I kept the ma'am and sir tradition with our own children, but with our grandkids they were allowed to say yes or no. Some days we reverted back to the ma'am and sir tradition when we saw that they were slacking in their manners. I can see how people can lose what society says is good manners, as each generation determine what to take from the previous one. One thing I learned from my big oops was to try and not make the same mistake again. My hope is that while our grandkids continue to decipher what manners to keep, and which ones to drop in their generation, that they will learn from their Oops.

The manners we modeled, and the good behaviors we encouraged in our kids were taught to prepare them for society. We said excuse me, thank you, sorry, or oops I goofed or made a mistake. So in turn we taught our children to say thank you when someone did something for them, to say thank you if someone gave them something, and to say thank you if someone gave them a compliment. We also taught our kids to say "excuse me" when they burped, passed gas, stepped on someone's toes or bumped into someone. As parents we felt such pride and admiration when we heard our kids recite most of these manners during their youthful years. We felt that we had given them a foundation that would indicate to the world that they were socially prepared, in the manners department. We were not sure if all of these manners transferred from inside our house to the outside world but realized that some of the things we taught our kids were passed down when we began to hear our grandkids use some of the same manners our kids were taught in their childhood.

I believe that certain manners are the fabric of "deterrence". No one wants to spend their life saying I'm sorry or oops! I goofed. So one only hope that in saying I'm sorry or oops! I goofed, that the mistakes that prompted those words would deter future ones. However, we find that in some cases it is not always what happens. As children age, I think that some of their manners fade as they develop their own set of rules and values. But what could be wrong with simple manners? What happens that people determine that simple manners of their youth could be exchanged for no manners to sometime manners? What happens to oops! I goofed? What happens to the excuse me? Are they rebelling against their parent's social values, or are the manners still there, and they are just not using them in their parent's presence. I wonder. Could it be that as parents we did not re-emphasize good manners as our kids matured? Did we not compliment or encourage them enough? Where do the lessons of previous oops go when they are faced with challenges such as stealing, giving in to peer pressure, cheating on test, or lying? Our hope as parents and grandparents is that the oops lessons of their youth will continue, and prevent them from having to say oops, I stole that, oops, I cheated, oops I lied. If the oops of their youth do not prevent them from doing things that they should not do, our hope is that it brings them to a place that allows them to show remorse, and eventually bring them back to the oops, and good manners that they learned.

Taking the Grandkids to school one morning, KeeKee stated, oops! I burped. As our eyes met in the rear-view mirror in acknowledgment, I thought to myself, please don't ever lose your Oops.

I DON'T LIKE CHILI'S

There aren't many restaurants that I don't like. When my husband and I got married, one of things we enjoyed most was going out to dinner. We have traveled to Germany, France, Italy, the Netherlands, Alaska and many other states in the United States. We have always found a good restaurant wherever we went. For many years we avoided going to Chili's because we thought it was more of a bar than a restaurant. We finally ventured out and visited one and it has become one of our favorite places to dine. When our granddaughter stated that she did not like Chili's, it reminded me of our first thought about the restaurant. We knew that once she tried it she was going to love it, like we do.

Teaching kids to feed themselves starts early. Not only does it free up the parents, but it provides the parents the opportunity to teach them etiquette skills when dining out. We were no different than any other parent in teaching our own kids how to act during a meal: sit up straight, talk quietly, don't yell, chew their food with their mouths closed, and say thank you. If they could learn those skills at home, we were almost assured that they would use them, and allow a family dinner outing to be an enjoyable one. Our kids had good "eating out" skills, and they used them as we tried to expose them to different kinds of food and restaurants. Let's fast forward to the Grandkids.

We wanted to introduce our Grandkids to Chili's, as we did not think they had ever been. TraTra stated, "I don't like this restaurant". When questioned as to why she did not like this restaurant, she indicated that is was because she wanted to go to McDonalds'. Once inside and seated, TraTra proclaimed to the waitress, I need to go to the bathroom. I assured the waitress that I would take care of this non-food need. A short time later the waitress asked if we needed anything, and TraTra stated to the waitress, "Excuse me, my tooth hurts". The waitress expressed her sorrow as she walked away. Did I mention in our set of instructions for eating out that you don't ask the waitress to take you to the bathroom, and that there is no dental care offered in the restaurant. Our grandkids, (I am not sure about anyone else's) are very vocal about what they want, and about what they do or don't like. It is this innocence that we tend to quiet or bring under control. But it is this innocence that instills bravery, and boldness. I believe that what we saw in the restaurant setting were kids displaying traits that they were taught from infancy: if you want something ask for it. At this age, they may not always be able to distinguish the right place, or right time to ask for their wants, but this boldness is what we have taught them. It is an opportunity to use it to introduce them to something new: a new food, or a new restaurant. It is also an opportunity to teach kids to try something at least one time before discounting it. By the time we left the restaurant, they were asking if we could come again. Chili's has become one of their favorite restaurants. Of course Grandparents usually has a vested interest in trying to convince someone to like something that they don't like: With Chili's being one of both of our favorite's, we frequent it quite often.

GOING TO CHURCH

When I think of church, one thing I think of, are the notes that I passed during the service, as we were not allowed to talk in church. What I know about church is that it was where I went to receive knowledge to build a solid foundation for my life based on the love of our Lord and Savior Jesus Christ. As we assist our daughter with our Grandkids, our hope is that they get the foundation we got. We know that most of the time they go to church to see their friends and eat doughnuts. We also know from what we have heard and seen from them that, like us they are absorbing what most of us get from Going to Church: building blocks for a solid foundation.

My husband and I were raised as Christians, and part of our belief as a Christian included weekly worshiping on Sunday in a Church. As parents we followed our parent's example and raised our family as Christians with the main worship taking place on Sunday as well. Fellowship was always an integral part of our worship experience, and it continues as such today. We began taking our grandkids to church when they were young. Sometime with their parents, but most of the time we would just take KeeKee. TraTra would occasionally come with us as well. We used our belief as a standard for teaching them about good and evil, about treating others respectfully. "What's respectful" TraTra asked? Respectful is treating people nicely.

As the years progressed, going to church on Sunday with Grandma and Papa became the norm for the two older girls. On the way home from church one Sunday, I asked them if they enjoyed church, and they said no that church was boring. The next Sunday they attended, I had gotten small tablets, and pencils for them to use during the service. They would write and draw in between the sits and stands of the church service. A month or so later, I wanted to find out if the girls were enjoying church any better. This Sunday, we had our usual fellowship; mingling, talking and eating. We usually have doughnuts as part of our fellowship. I asked if they enjoyed going to church any better, and they both said yes. Curious to find out what had made the difference, I asked them what had made them enjoy or like church now. They both blurted out the "doughnuts!" I am not sure that they understand, or care that this is not the real reason we are bringing them to church every Sunday. One could say that just being in Church will eventually pay off. One could also say that as kids we were the same way. We could sit through the Praise God, the Halleluiahs, and the songs of Zion, because we knew that there might be some refreshment in the back. But not to fear, all is not wasted, TraTra was singing a song she heard in Church, and she did not have the words quite right. KeeKee spoke up, and said, "that is not how that song goes" and proceeded to teach her the song. So, bring on the doughnuts (the wheat ones with less sugar), they "are" listening in church.

Occasionally on Sunday morning the two of them would say something that had to be written down for sharing. This particular Sunday the topic was again centered on doughnuts. TraTra started this dialogue with KeeKee:

Where are we going?
To Church.
What's Church?
It's a place where you eat doughnuts.
What are doughnuts?
Sweets.
What are sweets?
Sugar.
What is sugar?
Whatever?
What is whatever?
Leave me alone.

OK people, they are young, and understand who Jesus is, they know the Christmas story, they know right from wrong. So, give them time, they will understand it better by and by.

GRANDMA HE'S SPEEDING AGAIN

As we spent time with our grandkids we found them to be wiser earlier, and they had learned most of the age related items, and were ready for more. Teaching them to read road signs was a way of combating boredom on long trips. That knowledge came in handy on my trip to my Mom's house.

About five months after retiring from the Air Force, I decided that I would go home to North Carolina for a couple of weeks. I wanted to spend some time with my Mom before I started a new job. As usual, we take the oldest two grandkids with us when we go on vacation. I asked them if they wanted to go, and they said yes if they could go to Granny's house, and to the beach. They loved going to their Granny's house because they got to see most of their cousins, and they loved the beach. We usually go to West Virginia to visit our other grandkids while we are on vacation, but we were not able to on this trip. Normally when we go on vacation, my husband drives us, but he was unable to go on this trip, so we enlisted our Son to help with the driving. He would drive down, and then fly back, and my husband would fly down to drive us back. After tearful goodbyes (from the grandkids) we were on our way. I believe I saw their Mother run (well maybe increase her speed) to her van heading home for about a month of quietness. She had one child to care for instead of three at the time.

Our Son took the first leg of driving, as he was awake, and would be sleepy later. During our many trips with the grandkids, we had taught KeeKee how to read speed limit signs. She immediately started to use that skill as her uncle went over the speed limit. The trip takes about 15 to 16 hours, but we usually take longer as we stop, eat, and rest, especially when we take the girls. As my Son was driving, I napped in anticipation of my turn to drive. I awoke many times to the sound of Grandma, he's speeding again. The speed limit is 65, and I told him, but he ignored me. Besides we haven't even been to the beach or Granny's house yet, reported KeeKee. I reminded my Son that we were on vacation, and that we were in no hurry, so DON'T SPEED! Needless to say, after about 12 or 13 hours on the road, and on his second leg of driving, he was passing a car, and was over the speed limit. We heard the sirens and pulled over to the side of the road to receive our speeding ticket. Luckily the nice officer only gave him a warning and told him to slow down. My Son agreed, and for the rest of the trip, my napping was easier without the worry of him speeding. Their Mom called to see how the trip was going, and KeeKee again reported that they had not gotten her sea shells, not been to Granny's house, or the beach yet. She stated that we had not arrived at our destination because their uncle didn't know where he was going, and he was not using the GPS. Of course, the grandkids were getting tired of riding and began to "whine." That is usually our clue to stop and let them get out and stretch their legs.

AT GRANNY'S HOUSE

I was raised during the Baby Boomer years, and the Grandmothers I knew were called Grandma or Granny. The Grandfathers were called Grandpa or Granddaddy. I know that my family called them by different names so we would know which one we were talking about. As I entered the 20th century what Grandmothers were called began to change. In addition to the names above, I have heard them being called Ne Ne, G-Mom, Grandma-ma and GG. Going to one's grandparent's house usually meant lots affection, fun, and special sweets we didn't get at home. Just as I loved going to my Granny's house, our grandkids loved going to their Granny's house as well.

I was really looking forward to my vacation time with my Mom (Granny). This would give me the opportunity to make some memories with her, and the two granddaughters traveling with me. I ended up spending about three weeks with my Mom, and besides making memories, it afforded me the opportunity to give my sisters a rest, or break from taking her to the grocery store, doctor's office, or wherever else she needed to go.

Our own kids enjoyed going to visit my parents when they were smaller. They enjoyed playing in the open space, seeing, and playing with the animals, and they especially loved my Mother's cooking. I could never really sell them on the workings of the farm. They loved the fresh fruits and vegetables but did not like the work it took to get or prepare them. Even though, I did not like farm work, I found that I loved "shelling peas, and butterbeans".

While we were on vacation both girls wanted to comb their own hair, and dress themselves. KeeKee had spent one morning outside with her Granny in the flower bed. The following morning, she dressed herself in a dress instead of shorts or jeans. Both my Mom and I asked why she had put on a dress. She stated, "Granny has on a dress." Of course TraTra wanted to put on a dress too. My packing for the girls included jeans, shorts and church dresses. So, you can imagine trying to convince two dressed up little girls to change into shorts after they just watched my Mom play in the dirt in a dress!

Wearing a dress and not pants/shorts is a tradition bore out of religious beliefs, and it is still being observed by many today. I was only allowed to wear pants or shorts to play and work. We always wore dresses or skirts to school and church. I passed that tradition on to my daughter, until I realized that church was not about what you wore. I still tend not to wear pants to church on Sunday, and see nothing wrong about it, but it was ingrained during my youth, and I just never changed it. This is how families pass ideals, thoughts, cultures and traditions down to future generations. This is also how we maintain our ties with our heritage. As we grow and have our own families, it is up to us to decipher what works for us, and what does not and adjust as needed. After convincing the girls that it was ok to wear pants, they changed clothes that day, but wore skirts with shorts under them one day to play outside.

One of the things I wanted Mom to share with the girls was cooking, so we made a date to make Tea Cakes. This was our favorite dessert as kids, and Mom made them all the time. The girl's cousins came over, and they had so much fun making Tea Cakes with their Granny. Unlike my kids, they enjoyed shelling peas and butterbeans (like me), and they enjoyed going to the woods, and looking at trees with me. I knew they would want to spend most of their time outside, so I brought a tent to put out in the front yard for them to play in. At least it would keep some of the bugs, and the sun off of them. Even with the tent they got really tanned the three weeks we were on vacation.

Our trip to the beach was awesome. Luckily kids don't really care how far you drive to get to the beach, they just want water, sand and sea shells. My home state has beautiful beaches, and we have been to them many times. The beach is about a 2–3-hour drive from my Mom's house. On this visit home, we spotted a man-made lake that looked like a beach, and decided that we would go there. On beach day, we loaded up my sister's SUV, and headed to the beach (lake) with the grandkid's cousins. KeeKee had to be coached to go on the waterslide, but once she got the hang of it, she was unstoppable. TraTra kept yelling, "look Grandma, I'm swimming". She was crawling on the bottom of the lake! " I yelled back, great job." When it was time to leave, no one wanted to go. We promised them all that we would bring them back another day.

Two weeks into our vacation, TraTra packed her suitcase, drug it in into the living room and declared, "I am really ready to go home". Between my Mom's ahs, and my "we only have one more week to go," we were able to convince her to stay a little longer.

During our stay, I was really happy that the grandkids got to play with their cousins, visit with their aunts and uncles and spend quality time with their Granny. I wanted them to experience the same joy I had when I visited my Grandmother when I was a kid. They indicated that they had a good time, and when it was time to go, they cried, and did not want to go home. I knew I had accomplished my goal, as that is exactly how I felt every time when I had to leave my Granny's house.

WHAT DOES THAT MEAN?

I grew up with very little lingo or slang in our household. When I entered college, I began to hear a lot more, and had to think about what it meant. Being a concrete thinker, I generally do not think in abstract, and I am a very factual person. So, lingo and slang had to be interpreted by me, and by the time I understood it, the moment was gone. When the grandkids heard lingo from my generation, I could see their look of confusion. Lingo such as "You've got the big head" was literally translated by them as you have a big head. So included in a grandparent's job is translating lingo and slang.

As Grandparents, part of our role is teaching the next generation things we believe they will need to help them maneuver through this world. We used some of the same lingo we heard in our childhood, because for us, it worked to deter us from bad behavior. Some of that lingo worked on our own kids and, some did not, mainly because like our Grandkids, they did not understand what it meant. Kids and grandkids knew from the sound of one's voice that it was a good time to change their behavior when they heard certain lingo, whether they understood it or not. My husband is a master at using lingo from his childhood, but I don't remember my parents using a lot of it for deterrence. I have seen several books written that list the slang or lingo, and its meaning and there are lots of them. When the grandkids would require discipline, my husband would use words, or phrases of deterrence that was lingo driven from his childhood, and I would find myself explaining its meaning to them. Of course, by the time I was able to put into words they could understand the effect was gone. When he used phrases like "hard headed, acting up, or your eyes are bigger than your stomach" the grandkids had no idea what it meant. While he was using lingo, they are putting the true meaning to the words, and not really getting the meaning he intended. I asked my husband to use words or phrases that they could understand, and He's getting better.

Even though grandkids are smarter, more resourceful, and ingenious (SRI), I believe that weaving in some of the old lingo will help with future deterrence and will help them as they encounter the different generations who use lingo. They may not know what it means but coupled with tone and repeated explanations it can help encourage them to do the right thing.

In addition to using lingo to deter behavior, my husband and I have offered the grandkids advice on many things that we believed would help them in their daily lives. But what we learned in giving that advice that kids ARE SRI and can turn the advice you give into lessons for yourself.

We taught the girls to not answer the doorbell or respond to a knock on the door without permission. We explained that opening doors could be dangerous if you did not know who it was. I further explained that if they had to open the door to always ask "who is it? But the person may not be truthful, and could be a stranger. That is why adults should always open the door. KeeKee responded, Grandma, if you don't know who it is, I could just look through the window, and see who it is (our doors have side windows that one could just look out and see who is standing at the door). As I stood there listening to her solve a problem that I thought I was solving for her, I realized that our way, or advice is not always the best. The Bible indicates that "each generation will be wiser." What we have to realize is that our generation has to be open to receive wisdom, and change from the ones in front of us, our grandkids.

I had picked up KeeKee and TraTra from their house, and we were on our way to our house for them to spend the night. I needed to call my husband and tried numerous times to reach him on his cell phone. I must have tried to call him at least ten times. I explained to the girls the importance of carrying and answering a cell phone. In frustration, I commented, we could have had a flat tire, and been stranded on the side of the road before someone (Papa) called us back. KeeKee commented, Grandma if you have one flat tire, you still have three more. What is this wisdom called? A child shall lead them! If you have lemons, make lemonade! Don't let one flat tire stop the show! No it's that SRI thing!

I believed that thou shall not steal was an easy lesson to teach. We were helping our daughter raise the girls in the Christian faith. One of the principles we believe in is do not steal. Not only is this one of the 10 commandments, but it is common decency. KeeKee was being counseled on stealing candy (something that most of us have done). As adults, we believe that the voice of reasoning will whisper to us and deter us from doing something we should not do. So, I am thinking that my older granddaughter has matured to the point that she should be "hearing this voice". I asked her if she had heard a voice telling her not to steal when she was taking the candy. "Grandma, the only thing I heard was the noise of the air conditioner", and it's our candy, so how is that stealing. My daughter was listening to our conversation, and she had to leave the room to hide her laughter. I on the other hand had to keep mine hidden, as I was in front of her. I realized that this was not a good lesson to deter stealing. Hearing the voice of reason cannot be heard when you are five or seven years old (sometimes adults don't hear that reasoning voice).

There have been many opportunities for us as Grandparents to provide helpful hints or explain lingo to our grandkids. What I have learned is that we tend to over talk the advice we provide. I don't know when they stop listening, but I know they do. I also know that they hear the advice. I believe that we have to remember that this generation of kids is SRI and get our advice quicker. The longer we talk we are only satisfying our own egos, our own need to talk. They got the lessons minutes ago.

EPILOGUE

These two granddaughters have been so inspiring to watch as they grew and developed, and this is only a small glimpse of what they will be bringing to their generation. It feels good to know that as grandparents we have had the opportunity to influence them, and to be able to re-live those heartwarming experiences we had as kids through them. While grandparents only have a few stories to tell, think of what their parents would have to say. Well maybe not.

As I listen to RaeRae and EK, the youngest of their sisters (yes there are two more that live close by), interact with one another, I get the same feeling of inspiration, and pride to be a grandparent to them. Watching EK try and teach RaeRae, I can only imagine the stories they will provide. I believe that my last name will be Grandma for a long time to them as well. I now know that the word Grandma, Granny or whatever word is used, is not just about the word itself, but it is about the feeling they get when in the presence of a grandma or a grandparent. The same feeling, I had with my Granny.

Parenting children is a blessing. Grand-parenting children is an experience. One that I would not trade for anything in the world!

ABOUT THE AUTHOR

Ella Elliott Colvin was born in Grantham, North Carolina. She is married and she and her husband have three children, and six grandkids. She found that one of her greatest joys in the world comes from being a grandmother. She wrote this book to share just a portion of what she and her husband have experienced with the grandkid's other grandparents. A retired United States Air Force nurse, she has a Bachelor of Science degree in Nursing, a Master's Degree in Leadership, and a Retired Certification in Gerontology.

www.ingramcontent.com/pod-product-compliance
Lightning Source LLC
LaVergne TN
LVHW041639070526
838199LV00052B/3459